THE MEMPHIS SUN

THE MEMPHIS SUN

Jim Murphy

The Kent State University Press

Kent, Ohio, and London

for Glory

© 2000 by Jim Murphy
Library of Congress Catalog Card Number 00-0000
ISBN 0-87338-663-9
Manufactured in the United States of America

07 06 05 04 03 02 01 00   5 4 3 2 1

The Wick Poetry Chapbook Series is sponsored by the Stan and Tom Wick Poetry
Program and the Department of English at Kent State University.

Library of Congress Cataloging-in-Publication Data
Murphy, Jim, 1971–
    The Memphis sun / Jim Murphy.
        p.   cm.—(Wick poetry chapbook series two; no. 8)
    ISBN 0-87338-663-9 (pbk.: alk paper) ∞
    1. United States—Description and travel—Poetry.   2. National characteristics,
    American—Poetry.   I. Title.   II. Wick poetry chapbook series; ser. 2, no. 8.
PS3563.U738 M46   2000
811'.54—dc21   99-051690

British Library Cataloging-in-Publication data are available.

CONTENTS

ACKNOWLEDGMENTS

Grateful acknowledgment is made to *Painted Bride Quarterly, Brooklyn Review, Alabama Literary Review, Clackamas Literary Review, Yalobusha Review,* and *The Devil's Millhopper,* where certain poems in this collection have previously appeared.

I would also like to acknowledge the help of many friends in poetry, whose intelligence and camaraderie have been sources of inspiration at every step along this way.

ÉTUDES IN THE NEXT WORLD

Transcription flickers in the tallow light
while this practice room descends to sleep

then yields up just the yellowed bones.
The twentieth century's array of keys

will have to go unhammered now—so many
run-throughs have frozen all my fingers.

This must be territory near the bridge
Bill Evans crosses "Blue in Green,"

just without the lift from Chambers.
How am I supposed to know the changes

to be drawn out of this too-spare music?
Nowhere else to look and I don't recognize a thing.

DEPARTURES

MARSDEN HARTLEY PREDICTS
THE INTERSTATES

Square backs and air pressure—humid New York City
August afternoon that bears down on some sub-pavement dais
where news of the day has flattened out to pure abstraction.
Bats and pinstripes flash. Faces in ben-day dots get brushed
underfoot by gangs the same shades of burgundy and black.
Back in section B, Young Dwight Eisenhower drives a line
of tilting trucks deep into the mud of an Ohio road, and proves
the Wilson Administration maintains at least a sense of humor.
The green colonel's lost. Doors open with a bang. All directions
clang together, while pale men and women race the signals
for sandwiches and drinks, down toward the pneumatic hiss of brakes.

Marsden Hartley's at a corner table, outsized stopwatch
clicking off and on. The redcaps are Newtonian, hustling
behind luggage racks as they negotiate the crowd. This has to do
with art and speed, steps through the streamlines' flutes and curves.
His sketches of the trains are geometric fits—erratic rays,
loops and boxes that fill up every page. When waiting room
traffic vibrates down to the coffee in his cup, he looks out
to take in grades of color, the buzz of currents where
chalk cities meet and frantic talk booms up the concourse.
Too much time, too much, he thinks, these plans to make
each dull gray line undulate and surge from point to point.

ROUTES TO KANSAS CITY STAR

Roanoke Park to Rosedale Park, a few winding blocks
over to the angular disappointments of State Line Road,

none of it far from a garage studio where Thomas Hart Benton
collapsed and died at work, amid his spattered dropcloths

with a Royals' game crackling on the tin-foiled Radio King.
Sky of the plains tumbles over the bluffs' first knobs of green—

over Shawnee Mission, the blanks of Kansas City stockyards,
the three-forked river—two names that curl into a strain

of history like twin copperheads. Down in the sucking roots
botanic snarls break enormous chips off sidewalks

into dangled cement planes. Almost like the patched embroidery
of gray flannel uniforms, the Kansas City Monarchs

blazing through the bottom of the ninth, infield weeded
and full of gravel for shows of genius in leather-bare cleats—

around the diamond in twelve seconds, a six-hundred-foot home run,
two winning games pitched in an afternoon, whatever mystery

role was needed at the time—all ways to manage scenes—
the cue from Satchel Paige—*If a man can beat you, walk him.*

In the neighborhood of 18th and Vine, bad news
pours through almost every door, social club to barbershop

to clapboard church—*Can't pacify this mind of mine.*
Fogs of the "K.C. Blues" can't be kept so simple and free

this late in the dissipating day. F-stop, f-hole, twin-coiled
humbucking pickups—imagery pressed into coffee-table books

and scored in microgrooves. A Heavyweight Championship
of Blues Revue tacked to the lampposts and glued to the sides

of vacant buildings. Games in bottle gardens at midday.
I'm bumping around the block, same Carl Perkins number

running through my head—*sitting here wondering*
would a matchbox hold all my clothes. The laugh-while-you-can

catch of that is aimed in this direction. The sod country's
mud runs high through Lawrence on its Biblical approach.

The street's clouded over by the time I shamble up and talk
to the vendor. I'm in my role. He's in his. *Hey buddy,*

how much? Two bits, pal. The orchestrated casting off
of boredom—the heavy sky, the late game, the mayor's race.

A block down thinking *What'd I want with this?*
Classifieds. "Marketplace." A make-do hat for the rain.

MOMENTS WITH MS. GOLIGHTLY

White cake and glass after glass of dry champagne.
      My face must be shining. Do you feel warm?

It's not what she says, what she says when she reaches
      the Magnavox console and drops another stack

of brand new 45s on the plastic spindle. *You know*
      I love these little things. I'm not sure

just what she means. *If you could be anywhere*
      in the world, where would you be?

Outside, someone checks his watch and stumbles
      with an armload of gladiolas through the downpour.

Another mouthful's too much. My cheeks must look nice
      bulging with booze. Big mistakes. *How's that?*

Like Dizzy Gillespie. *I'd be right here. With you.*
      (With her, forty years of calendar scenes,

on film shot backwards. Forty Decembers—
      freezing drizzle in our faces. Mascara so heavy

we streak as the string section swells and kettledrums roll
      through the soundtrack of each washed-out frame.

In the negative, you can clearly see the cheek bones
      of her perfect face.) *And we're here now.*

All of this she's said without a single glance toward me,
      trying to decide on Percy Faith or Billie Holiday.

Turning the sleeves in her too-sharp hands
      as if to judge them, she waits for what I have to say.

INVISIBLE PHILADELPHIA

1

In Rittenhouse Square, a white man pirouettes
behind a wrought iron fence—*No paparazzi*

running after me! No pictures, please!

No one on the path could guess his age,
much less recall the features of his face.

The evening's docile as a sleeping dog.

Even the sergeant coming across the street
doesn't hurry. He's staring through the scene.

2

I wanted that church thing up in my music.

Like a fool, I underline the passage.

I can't remember whose idea it was
to separate in a city we don't know.

A sudden gust blows pages, pens and napkins
almost off the glass. I slam both hands

on the table just to keep these things in place.
Of course, the coffee spills all over me.

And then the longest limousine on earth
spreads around the corner and up the street.

Its windows reflect a panoramic view
of storefronts through the humid, July haze,

so people on the curb can see themselves—
Tight T-shirts, cartoon puffs of smoke

across their chests. Japanimation scenes
while the comic sweat pops off my brow.

3

The most spiritual saxophonist
in history is high on the beams
of the Walt Whitman Bridge.
                              But memory
won't place him there, bending to be near
some idea of solace—that Love Supreme.

The syncopated clank of tension wires
above the oily Delaware, the sleeping
gulls in rows like stiles, the slow red pulse
that cuts the minutes up,
                              the single look
across the span, the wordless handing down
and stepping back so someone else can take
the lead, the sigh, and tightening of the reed.

4

Snow's falling again outside the theater—
huge crystals of it vanish in well-done hair
and on good shoes. Some are shifting weight,
stamping feet, some have their arms around
each other. I blab some half-remembered lines
about South Street and nudge you in the ribs.
Thank God the dinner wine we chose was strong.
But we won't have to wait much longer.

                                        In front,
double doors swing open, and people press
to glimpse the leather-suited figure now
emerging from a car. He doesn't wave,
just ducks the flashbulbs bursting all around
and disappears inside. Not much for us
to say, until you show me what I missed—
Did you see that? He carried his own case.

TRANSACTIONS UNDER GLASS

Why not let the whole morning turn on the brick cylinders
      that ring the one-room war museum?

Why not have the bed that he was born on be the index?

Through small gaps in the cabin walls, the whisper of a pencil . . .

Precursors unnerving as mice, someone destined to have
      his image made and made again.

This popular history consists of flattened lead
      recovered from the trunks of white oaks in Tennessee,
a bed too small for the President to bleed on,

all linked to someone else—a man with his spur caught
      on the bunting who shouts

sic semper tyrannis

in slow motion for eternity. Nervous laughter. He himself
      is hauled off through the mezzanine.

·

More intimate with the green web of Lincoln's face
      than the print of my own thumb.

·

It would be nearing four o'clock by now—
      a window of ideal light marked by charcoal on the sill.

Face lit with spectral color, she's seated with a whalebone prop
      behind her head—slow daguerreotype exposure.

The process yields a cloudless two-inch likeness
        that can be wiped from the plate with a finger.

The practitioner stinks of fried river fish, breathing
        in her face, pulling on her chin.

His fingers on her temples, eyes met, then a nod
        that's supposed to be assurance.

He's striding backwards. One hand floats out, the other
        reaches for the black cap covering the lens.

The sitter gapes at a gray horizon drawn on paper
        and all her second thoughts are gone.

It's the cost of luxury. You can see her sidled up to death,
        having cleared her throat for nothing.

CHARLES BON CONSIDERS HEAVEN

I must admit, the bravura of fine music has never moved my blood.
I prefer the plainness of the bugle call at dawn, the measure
of confinement in a parlor cello. Some draw sudden breath
for the weave of chamber music, or for the complex circles
that comprise a symphony. These bewilderments are brothers
to the cough of the cart vendor. In effect they are very close.

But the endless cadence of our feet, the drum at the close
of day beyond our evening fires—these quietly boil my blood
and seem to diminish without dying, like peals of a bell. My brother
still sleeping in his hammock cannot hear them. I measure
the distance we've marched by the stars. And if a mountain's circle
or a tree crown cuts the sky, I just listen to Henry's breaths

and stoke the embers with a stick. It's comic how my breath
goes short at a rustle of leaves, or at an owl's screech close
to camp, when I've never once felt afraid in combat's circle
of lead and cracking timber. The sight of my own blood
becomes a simple nuisance; but I don't pretend a scratch measures
my courage against the dead's. Henry and I are lucky brothers

who yet laugh and take shots at quail from horseback, brothers
as we were in peace. On otherworldly afternoons, we saw the breadth
of Rampart Street alive with mirror pools. We poured measures
of cold rum punch and beer because the steam and sun hung so close.
We toasted law, marked the quality of horses, sliced and ate blood
oranges. Henry approved all, swinging his drinks in imperfect circles.

I won't defend my choices to conceal whole figures, to encircle
him with closing doors and arches. I had no means by which a brother
could be made, no way to introduce him to the fact that we were blood.
I pointed out his face in mirrors, and never let his voice give breath
to any doubts in me, tried to let this wash of alcohol and war close
off his memory. We traded topcoats and identities, his error measured

larger with each wink and shoulder clasp. Those necessary measures
bound his life to mine. But these nights under stars, when circles
of the dead surround us sleeping, when I feel their imposition close
around us, hissing through the grass, then I am truly Henry's brother,
no less than any living man, and I'm satisfied that the monotony of breath
itself is music, the pulse that moves like a slow metronome in my blood.

To joke, they say that by your breath is how a good day's measured
here. They circle cities on a map and talk about how close
we are to victory. Every face ash gray, blood gone. My brothers.

JUNK TRAVEL THROUGH WEST MEMPHIS

Woman with a starshell light behind her eyes
turns slowly on the sugar of a ride cymbal,
and moves her hands toward the Pleiades

she imagines strung across the dancehall floor.
Other hands are soft on her white taffeta,
and the fingers everywhere in her things

only add their flashing brushes to the torsion.
What a love this is, at the core of quiet music
where rings and wallet can be gladly given over.

Shoes, too, and a bracelet with eight red stars
swinging from the band are offered to those most
interested in need. Her frayed hem sweeps up,

and the bassist at his hat rack lifts an arm
to the backward-rushing bride. She unfolds
the packet of her tin-foil heart, invites each one

to touch it. She wants them all at her cotillion.
What matters is the glow around her mansion,
though the eaves are overrun with Spanish moss

and the portico is strewn with broken glass.
The alloy in her brain's blood shimmers—
she slips and taps inside its iridescent wave.

ARRIVALS

STONE DOVES OF WILLIAM EDMONSON

Nashville, 1937

They suit for bath or grave. Anywhere under the sun,
up front in the azaleas, or near the green shelves
of moss and terraced mushrooms—his birds are there.
Twin doves gauge the cracked basin and contemplate
each other yard-high above the runneled ground.
They hail the carver at each glimpse of morning.
He sees their shapes as coffee steam drifts from a tin cup
he carries spider-fashion through the door.

You get the call, you got to move

Second Monday, the men from Ezell Mill and Stone
pile cast-offs at the foot of his drive, pieces small enough to carry.
This blunt one—a Carolina panther's head. The jagged sliver—
nose of alligator gar. But just this one round bit of lime
has the rapid heart that pumps the chest of a bird.
Edmonson, chisel on a roll, lifts the whole woods,
pulls the blue down here, where we can hear the knock.

Come from the High Hand

And a fist assembles—each eye and feather groove
pressed by tools still specked with varnish from a run-off year.
When it's ready for the march to vaults on Ararat, the dove
tilts on the hand-pinched turret, as if it could spring down.

He takes my mind off it, tells me I got work to do

Phrase for graveyard carriage. Tomorrow, drained balm
jars and broken pots will hem the grave. One will set
a smashed fiddle down against the marker, say a word
and turn to go. The dove's glass eye will radiate

a while as it glitters in its place. A few years in the glue,
then down to the knotted runners, the plot no one
keeps clean. Shorted all this time, but that's not the point
where birds shoot through a notch in towering cedar.

He hung a tombstone out for me to make

THE CONTINENTAL'S GAMING TABLES

Plush Pullmans rumble through the gaps,
tables littered with the oldest desert myths.

On a matchbook, King Solomon's got him
by the heels, ready for an explanation.

Nebuchadnezzar's downfall is embossed
in Greek on the back of the daily special.

The gamblers in their deep blue finery
are seated always at the middle of the car,

trick bags full and empty, shrugs and shells.
These travelers are talking, drinking fast

far into the night, hands shaken all around.
Ugly fortunes fall from bitten lips—

a six of hearts, a glass cat's eye, tumbler
full of sympathy, electroplated ticket-punch,

ballpoints, dreambooks, a rotten tambourine,
historic dates printed on a stippled skin.

The cars lunge forward, left and right,
rounding mountains, shouldering oceans,

far into mazes of a green and gray landscape,
unsteady compulsions and the drumming rails.

FLORIDA RESORT SCENE, 1964

A number one record warping in the April sun—
monaural air raid speakers in the eaves
corrupt the hits but no one cares. All the blue
green and gray around the water has gone
white electric with the spike of sudden fame.
One of them lifts a *mai tai* from a silver tray
and toasts the *maitre d'* with an awkward clink
against the bottom of someone's half full Coke.
The Herald's starched features photographer
has arrived just in time. He squints and shuffles,
raises his hands and cranks the roll, trying candids,
trying to avoid the cross-eyes and lunatic grins
when they're caught in ticklish conversations.
It's all been hard to understand. The buck-toothed one
in madras shorts looks a bit unstrung. He's having
his pink back aloed by three women in bikinis.
He cringes and rolls his head around, crying for
a doctor, a vicar, and another drink. Busboys
are covering the aftermath of a buffet in tin foil,
sneaking cufflinks and signed papers into pockets.
One of the help twists around, starts to down
a warm beer and gets clapped hard on the shoulder.
Wot's all this lot then? What was that? English?
It's the thinnest one of them, dripping in a velour robe,
wiping hair and water from his eyes. He was seen
on color TV, trading fake punches with the champ
while the others begged and moaned for mercy.
Now the swim has worn him down. He's fumbling
for a pack of Dunhills, all smile and yellow teeth.
It's two o'clock, and already the scene is packing.
A pissed off *someone* barks into a creamy telephone
tethered to the golden patio. Is it Murray the K?
A rock 'n' roll old man, walking heart attack?
The fourth one, treading water, slaps a wave

of chlorine cool in his direction, and the entire crowd
erupts with laughter: all the local TV stars
and quiz bowl winners, lucky radio call-in girls
who have hidden behind their wingtip glasses,
the Stetsoned steak house owner, hip Cadillac
dealer, Ann-Margret in a lovely pastel sundress,
all the formerly bored waiters, the sleepy beatnik
disc jockey who needs to pop amphetamines,
the crew-cut president of Sigma Alpha Epsilon
and his fabulous date decked out in polka dots,
the proud mayor with his misprinted city key,
somebody's boss, the sheriff, the crippled boy
and blind girl warming to it all, the mothers
with jumpy hearts and instamatic cameras,
desperate for this one pure day of joy, all of them
crowding tighter, closer for the opening
and final line as the Beatle smiles, bows
deep at the waist, and slips his body down.

WHAT MAKES TODAY'S COLD KITCHEN

A woman played harp in purple flannel
in the corner of my kitchen Sunday morning.

I swear. Her lips were pressed tight to the slots,
and the music from her breath made a sound

like blades on glass. Someone set the teapot
on the gas. Someone pulled up the shade

that crossed off another day from August
courtesy of Quaker State. Dawn broke

always like it does—blue flame and static
cranked into gear. Her hands were cupped

around a tune about another town.
Room for a decade's worth of blues to pass

between each verse. It didn't matter who
I was—monkey-man or senator.

She never said before she left. I turned,
and the light fell on what I'd missed—some rain

or a break-in, someone's windshield scattered
like road salt, all across an empty space.

VICTORY THEATER

for Richard Estes

The marquee almost comes alive when sun
hits the curtain wall that fills our field of vision.
It's punctured like the side of a steamship
with galleries and portholes—a bit derelict,
but true to the velvet palace's original dominion:

comfort and escape. In front, a vinyl garland
of flags announces the apparition of blue skin
that mercilessly shakes inside. At half past six
        the marquee almost comes alive.

Look at 42nd Street's tacked-on sophistication
frozen in the hi-gloss of a summer afternoon.
The painted theater is real as any technicolor epic.
And without a single turning wheel to break the quiet,
you can step back from the curb and see it's 1961.
        The marquee almost comes alive.

GIFT AND PRIZE

Manners still intact, smack of poor talk
sparking on our lips—mid-afternoon
rain makes the roof tiles steam across
the empty rows of streets. The parkway
is so far and unconnected from us now
that traffic seems to be a sound from
some other century. We may never play
the Charlie Patton 78 we found this morning
for sale on two sawhorses and a door.
Its silver-blue sleeve promises a knockout,
but we'll have to put it in our book and wait
to see if what's on the brittle wax still swings.
These gifts are simple, held in one hand
up to the light and rattled hard for soundness.
For the right ones we're ready to break the bank,
as if the mementos we devote our spare time to
collect and endlessly nail up as evidence
were all free for the asking. Paper money,
case of wine, wall of books—all free. Our luggage
sits in a pool of rainwater. We sag on the split
gray lip of a bench, and I have to pull you
close just to feel that you're still there.
Even the green mountains can go to hell.
For the shameless moment, I covet my own life.

ELMORE JAMES STEPS OUT OF
A STALLED CAR

Careful not to curse the steaming pile of rust, himself,
or the whole snow-blurred city of Detroit, Elmore James,
true king of the bottleneck guitar, whispers something calm
and noncommittal as he jams the floor brake down
with style and force. He has time to shove back
the sleeve of his long London Fog and look at his Timex
before the real mess starts. This rearview vision of her
body fidgeting—always too hard to please—
at the moment about to break on cue into tears,
soon as his arm comes over back of the bench
and he slowly cranes his neck around to see.

•

And none-other-than Elmore James runs a hand along the rim
of his torn-up porkpie hat, wiping this winter scene
all the way back to the fissured roads north of Mobile—
shells and bright ceramic shards, flints and stray coins always
catching eyes along every unmanned stretch of blacktop in the South.

Flat foot, flat top, rag top—evolution of the phony contract,
trucking state to state. Always some blank face to look into,
tapping fingertips barely in from the grasshopping glare.
You play that thing, hanh? What bad news next?
Must not know how to work, I guess.

•

Steps past corrugated, flung-off roofs, rust-and-rainwater–mottled
ribs of some foundation, charcoaled apse of a burned church
blown through as if struck by siege cannon, hiss of the grub worms
working in the framework of a thousand family homes.

Light that comes stealing up behind a rise, night and day
all rolled-over—one morning like a boot in the back, some other
dawn when all the cool that simmers off by noon stays close
and straightens the thousand roads out with its blue kisses.

Opened the door on backseats stocked with stacks of zip guns,
baseball gloves and boxes of cigars—everything for sale
from new 45s up to works of Shakespeare, pocket-size, some "frenchy"
playing cards, even dresses with a horse sewn on the pocket.

·

And this was all he brought back to the city for his only girl.
Brought back in the icebound Buick from Alabama to Detroit
one horsey dress, white leggings and a pair of buckle shoes,
the reason why Elmore James steps out of a stalled car to the sound
of screaming almost happy, with no tricks to figure out but
what to say about the hour, and location of the nearest phone.

MISSING MEMPHIS' DESIRE SIGNS

Up from the hollow storefronts and caverns
        in cinder block that trapped sounds coming off the river,
some projects stood half-finished, empty halls perfect
        only for smoking, for random persons walking through.
The individuals in question broke wide open in Memphis
        and proceeded unapprehended into myth,
calico dress and Nudie suit streaming through the drowse
        of lights that panned across the interstates.

•

Some child wasting time, shooting bottle rockets
        from a motel balcony in Winona might not know
a thing about it, but for some there is a pattern in the way
        it all turns out. This system leads our heroine
to the bottom of a bottle, to places where she won't embrace
        the slips of friends who suddenly profess love—
strange confessions made on sofas, abrupt kisses between
        bad silences, all the wrong things once again.

•

"You're Right, I'm Left, She's Gone"
        bubbled up from under the pavement on Union Avenue.
Those at the source must've shared some misunderstanding,
        some desire to fix their age, and not even wax-faced Jesus
on the dashboard or the smile of an opaque hula girl
        could've kept their wheels from slipping. What a joke
each time the bad luck stories start—no man or woman
        could have made this love go right.

•

But here they are again, before their fall from Grace.
        Here's love coming live with forty-thousand watts—

why not—*from the Delta to the stratosphere*—
  for those endless clear November nights
when somebody's cut loose for the first time,
  wallet full of twenties, watching for the mileage signs
beside the southbound highway—a road jammed full
  with thoughts of people bound for Memphis.

SOME PERSONAE

MARSDEN HARTLEY (1877–1943), American painter whose work reached its apogee in pieces such as *A German Officer* (1914, New York, Metropolitan Museum of Art). Hartley's experiments in highly abstracted form and bold color are part of a broad-based reaction to technology and speed found in arts of the modern era.

HOLLY GOLIGHTLY, a central character in Truman Capote's *Breakfast at Tiffany's* (1958), portrayed by Audrey Hepburn in the 1961 film version.

CHARLES BON and HENRY SUTPEN, fictional half-brothers created by William Faulkner to explore the limits of loyalty and identity in *Absalom, Absalom!* (1936).

WILLIAM EDMONSON (?–1951), American vernacular sculptor who began making funerary art after thirty years of labor in railroad shops at St. Louis, Chattanooga, and Nashville, following a vision of God. Supported in part by the Tennessee WPA Art Project, in 1937 Edmonson was the first black artist to have a solo exhibition at the Museum of Modern Art in New York. A fine study of Edmonson's work is found in John Michael Vlach's *By the Work of Their Hands: Studies in Afro-American Folklife* (Charlottesville: University Press of Virginia, 1991).

RICHARD ESTES (1936–), American painter of the photorealist school who, unlike many others in this mode, paints by hand instead of with an airbrush. His *Victory Theater* (1968, The Detroit Institute of Arts) depicts the now-resurgent Times Square theater in a less prosperous period.

ELMORE JAMES (1918–1963), American blues guitarist whose version of Robert Johnson's "Dust My Broom" is a landmark in the development of slide, or "bottleneck," style. James was a regular player on KFFA's *King Biscuit Time*, Sonny Boy Williamson's program broadcast from Helena, Arkansas for more than twenty-five years.